# Wish You Were 'Here!

## COLORING BOOK

## TERESA GOODRIDGE

### DOVER PUBLICATIONS
### GARDEN CITY, NEW YORK

This charming collection invites colorists to tour the world. Each of the 31 picturesque images features a different locale, from a quaint seaside town, a relaxing beach, and a snowy ski resort to a romantic gondola ride in Venice, a spectacular safari in Africa, and a breathtaking view of the Taj Mahal. These beautiful postcard scenes will delight both experienced and armchair travelers! Plus, each of the illustrations is perforated for easy removal and display.

*Copyright*

Copyright © 2020 by Dover Publications
All rights reserved.

*Bibliographical Note*

*Wish You Were Here! Coloring Book* is a new work,
first published by Dover Publications in 2020.

*International Standard Book Number*

*ISBN-13: 978-0-486-84540-1*
*ISBN-10: 0-486-84540-0*

Manufactured in the United States by LSC Communications
84540002
www.doverpublications.com

2 4 6 8 10 9 7 5 3

2021